CONTENTS

What is an API, in "English Please"?..3

Introducing APIs...4

THe Business Case for APIs..5
    Integrating external APIs in your product 6
    Building and using APIs for internal product connectivity...6
    Building and exposing APIs for your product to external world 7

What is an API? I am ready for some actual understanding now. 8

Request Response Cycle 10
    Requests and Responses 10
    EXTENSIBLE MARKUP LANGUAGE (XML)...11
    JAVASCRIPT OBJECT NOTATION..12

Types of APIs 15
    Ownership types of Web APIs..15
    Communication level of APIs 16

Web service APIs 18
    SOAP...18
    JSON-RPC and XML-RPC..19
    REST 19

Common HTTP Methods (REST) 20
    ENDPOINT 20
    GET..21
    POST...22
    PUT..22
    DELETE..23

Response Codes...25

API Documentation 26
    Types of API Documentation...27
    API Documentation Structure...28

Work with an API (LIVE Example) 29

Other API Terminologies 35
    API Calls 36

    Payloads 36
    Headers 36
    Authentication 36
    OAuth 37

API Testing & Monitoring 38
    API Testing and why should you care? 38

Bonus 39
    List of fun APIs 39

References 40

Phew, I know enough - what to do with this info? 41

WHAT IS AN API, IN "ENGLISH PLEASE"?

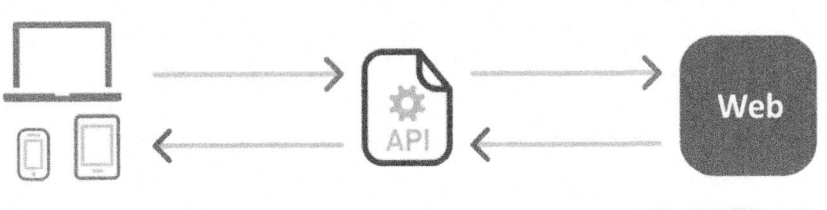

> An API(Application Programming Interface) is simply something that sends information back and forth between an application, website and a user.

Imagine back in the day, before cell phones. You had a crush on someone, but you were too shy to talk to them face to face. Let us say you wrote a note and sent it through a friend to them. Your friend takes your message to them, gives them the message, and brings back a response from them.

In this example, your friend is the API. You stay where you are. Your crush stays where they are. Your friend brings your message to them, and then brings their response back to you.

It is really that simple (may not have been while writing that note to them though :p)

Now that you know, what it is and are not turned off by the word "API" anymore, let us talk about everything else.

As product folks, we are often referred to as "the techie" by business stakeholders, sales, marketing and management. However, we are still looked down upon by our actual tech friends from the Dev, QA DevOps teams when it comes to anything technical.

Technology skills are part of the holy trinity of Product Management skills: business, technology, design. Not all of them may be essential and in-depth knowledge is never a target. However, the understanding of business, technology and design certainly helps strengthen decision-making. The amalgamation of these skills allows measuring tradeoffs and clarifying potential business opportunities when used appropriately.

Which creates a good case for getting under the tech hood. Enter APIs.

INTRODUCING APIS

Of all the technologies that a Product Manager could soak up, APIs seem to solve the most burning need, because of their versatility. APIs have become one of the most common tools in product creation and scale up as they significantly expand the product attributes and possible business opportunities.

Did you know?

Netflix can stream to over 800 different device types thanks to its API.

Ebay delivered more than 1 billion PPE items since April 2020 with its API services

Ebay serves 150-250 million API hourly calls

2.8 billion API requests are processed by GitHub per day

1 Billion API Calls from Corporate Clients are processed by CitiGroup's Digital Channels

 **Open any ecommerce app/site and search for something**

Let us look at a basic Amazon Page. Imagine you were to shop for an Alpaca soft toy (just because). If you take a moment to notice the components of the Amazon web page (I have highlighted only some important ones), you will realize it is not a simple web page. It is built on various components that probably are individual products and you may spot some of that elsewhere too. Like the Social Media Integration, or location (Amazon could or could not have built this on their own, but if they could instead create simple APIs to external products, why would they build on their own?)

Each of the pieces indicated by the red boxes exposes an API that is consumed by the team building the ecommerce site. The Product Managers building those products (some internal APIs, some external) made a business decision to open their API and allow others to integrate. They had a vision in mind on how it would be used in tandem with other businesses and the value it would bring to their direct and indirect users.

As a product manager, understanding an API can help with various business decisions, like including an open API as part of your product or consuming one. These decisions could provide an advantage that can boost the success of your product. There are also significant business challenges that come with working with APIs, and as a Product Manager, one must consider and be prepared.

THE BUSINESS CASE FOR APIS

For a product you are building, APIs could be leveraged in multiple ways:

- Integrating with external APIs
- Building and using APIs for internal product connectivity
- Building and exposing APIs for your product to external world to leverage information or functionalities from your product

 Imagine you are building a note-taking app like Evernote, Google Keep, TableNotes or something else of your fancy

Let us talk about the pros and cons of each of the above through this example.

Integrating external APIs in your product

What if you wanted to save video notes in your imaginary Notes App, while you were working on an important topic like APIs. Here, there could be two ways to do this: either create a whole logic, interface etc. in the app to display, upload videos or integrate an external API like YouTube API by just integrating based on their API logic.

The latter approach can fast track your 'brainstorm to build' time. Features that you and your team will take considerable time to create can be made available to your users simply by integrating with any existing service/product of your choice. This can also add a flair to your otherwise simple boring product by just integrating some fancy functionalities.

Pros: Shorter lead times, low maintenance overhead, additional functionality to end consumers resulting in enhanced user experience

Cons: Your product now depends on something you or your team cannot control. Any enhancements/ customizations will depend upon the availability/flexibility that the borrowed API can provide. Cost could vary depending on the third party product and may impact your cost to end customers. Also, the fear of losing the functionality altogether that may impact end user value remains.

Many products today utilize integrations with APIs. Here are few examples of open APIs that are widely used:

- Google Maps API
- Payment Gateways (PayPal, Stripe, GPay, etc.)
- Google Calendar APIs
- CRM APIs like Zoho, Salesforce

Building and using APIs for internal product connectivity

Let us say the Notes App you created is fabulous. It sells really well and is technically stable, so you decided to launch another digital product, an email service like Gmail.

One of your former clients now wants to buy this second product. You want to make the combination of these even better for the clients, so you ask the dev team to allow users to be able to email their notes with a combination of both products.

In this case, your technical team will build APIs to interface both product to allow the notes app to share data to the email app using an API. Your client will experience one seamless integration and you benefit from both products.

Some general examples of this scenario can be like you integrating posting your Instagram stories to Facebook just by logging in to the Facebook application.

Pros: Seamless flow of information. Uninterrupted experience for end user

Cons: Dependencies on internal infrastructure, capability of teams

Building and exposing APIs for your product to external world

Your Note taking app is already popular and it is possible that some users want to use these notes in their calendar, so that they don't forget their action items. Here, in order to facilitate the user requirements you create an API of your Notes application that allows to exchange data with other popular Apps.

This alternative is often discussed, when you are on your path to building a scalable/self-sufficient ecosystem for your product. This will be a crucial decision that may fall in your bucket post technical feasibility. Here's where the business viability should be evaluated. Building and exposing an API for your application will depend on what your product is. If it is a service that cannot survive without an integration like a Payment gateway, you will need to create and share your APIs for your business.

If it is something that's just good to have but has some demand from customers, you can evaluate what the product appetite suggests for the API.

Pros: Could give your product immense boost by partnering with other products, or sharing the added value to your clients

Cons: Maintenance, security, API architecture design framework

WHAT IS AN API? I AM READY FOR SOME ACTUAL UNDERSTANDING NOW.

An Application Programming Interface, or API, is a technology that connects two systems. As explained earlier, APIs allow two systems to communicate with each other.

Let us take another example: In the pre-digital era, you go to the library and are looking for 'Rich Dad, Poor Dad' by Robert Kiyosaki. However, the library is like the library of congress and you have no clue where to find this book.

What do you do?

The quickest and most efficient way is to reach out to the librarian handling the huge catalog, which has the list of books, their details, location and availability to borrow. You request for your book 'Rich Dad Poor Dad' from their list. The librarian looks up the catalogue to check some details, walks through the labyrinth of shelves to find the book and brings it to you.

Great, your job is done.

In this example:

Library	The database, which is one of the systems involved and is restricted to outsiders to protect data integrity
Books	The data/information that will be shared.
You/ Customer	The requestor, the application/system looking for information
Librarian	The API of course, they take your request, go to the database and return back to the requesting application with the desired information
Request for the book	The call made to the API or better known as the Request
Catalog	Specific format the request/call has to follow so that the API understands it (API Documentation or specification)
Book you received from the librarian	The response for your request

This is what an API does: it acts as the interface between two applications and facilitates information transfer while ensuring all defined technical standards like speed and security. Or is essentially an agreement between two applications and the API documentation determines the terms of the agreement.

If everyone asks for a book in their own way, the librarian will not be able to fulfill the requests; hence, APIs are designed to a specification that must be followed by all the systems requesting information.

REQUEST RESPONSE CYCLE

When I hear about APIs, I also come across request response, JSON, REST, what is all that?

Coming to that, now that we understand the basics of an API, we will focus on some key things that would give us a good breadth of information on APIs and their ecosystem:

- Requests and responses
    - XML and JSON
- Types of APIs
    - REST
    - HTTP methods
- Endpoints
- API documentation
- API calls
- Payloads
- Response codes
- Headers
- Authentication

Requests and Responses

We understand in layperson's language, when talking about an API, what a request and response means. Referring to our Library example, Request was the 'Ask' for a book and response was the book. Before we delve deeper, let us look at two other terminologies that will come in handy.

- XML and
- JSON

In order for two systems to communicate with each other, there needs to be a standard (like English language for some humans). If two websites have to communicate between each other, they can create a standard of their own based on specific parameters that need to be exchanged. But, how would you standardize this for others, other unknown parties? Especially, between plethora of websites, applications, systems wanting to exchange information with hundreds of different types of parameters.

How would you do it?

Well, this is the problem that both XML and JSON solve.

EXTENSIBLE MARKUP LANGUAGE (XML)

Let's walkthrough an example of what XML looks like. This is modified from this XML file on W3Schools. It's made delicious so that you can focus on the example.

```xml
<?xml version="1.0" encoding="ISO-8859-1"?>
<breakfast_menu>
    <food>
        <name>Waffles</name>
        <price>$5.95</price>
        <description>
        two Waffles with chocolate syrup
        </description>
        <calories>650</calories>
    </food>
    <food>
        <name>Strawberry Waffles</name>
        <price>$7.95</price>
        <description>
        light waffles
        with blueberries and whipped cream
        </description>
        <calories>900</calories>
        <sides>
            <side>
            <name>Sausage</name>
            <price>$2.00</price>
            </side>
            <side>
            <name>Bacon</name>
             <price>$2.50</price>
            </side>
        </sides>
    </food>
</breakfast_menu>
```

In this example, we have menu items, where the second item has extra sides. XML generally starts with a line stating the version and encoding of the document (there are tons of options), and it has tags that detail out parts of the document, with details of content inside them.

XML can also be formatted to use tag attributes, let us see the same example with tag attributes:

```xml
<breakfast_menu>
<food name="Waffles" price="$5.95" description="two Waffles with chocolate syrup" calories="650">
</food>
<food name="Strawberry Waffles" price="$7.95" description="light Waffles with blueberries and cream" calories="900">
        <sides>
                <side name="sausage" price="$2.00"/>
                <side name="bacon" price="$2.50"/>
        </sides>
</food>
</breakfast_menu>
```

Makes it look neater. That's it. That's all you need to know about XML for now. Nothing to be scared of. Just a simple way of structuring data and parameters.

JAVASCRIPT OBJECT NOTATION

XML is great and has been around for a long time. However, one drawback that the dev community has been vocal about is that it is slightly cumbersome with too many characters. In some ways, data can also be compressed and formatted in a particular way that XML and JSON look similar. JSON and XML can be interchangeable, although many developers prefer to use JSON over XML.

The above delicious example in JSON could look like this:

```
{
  "name": "Waffles",
  "price": "$5.95",
  "description": "two Waffles with chocolate syrup",
  "Calories": "650",
},
{
  "name": "strawberry Waffles",
  "price": "$7.95",
  "description": "light Waffles with blueberries and cream",
  "Calories": "900",
}

  "sides": [
    {
      "name": "sausage",
      "price": "$2.00"
    },
    {
```

```
    "type": "bacon",
    "number": "$2.50"
  }
 ]
}
```

Notice that JSON is simply JavaScript objects, or hashes, with "keys" and "values." Another standard of sharing data between systems. Again, that's enough information for us for now ☺

Coming back to the request and response cycle, API works like we talked about, using 'request' and 'response'. A user requests something in a specific format as outlined in the API documentation (XML/JSON) like we just saw and the API responds with something in return.

For example, using the Instagram API I can request a list of posts on cute alpacas (Yes, I'm obsessed)

 Open Instagram or Facebook App – Pull Down OR Type "Cute Alpacas" or anything else that you like and hit search

When you did as described in the activity, this is what happened:

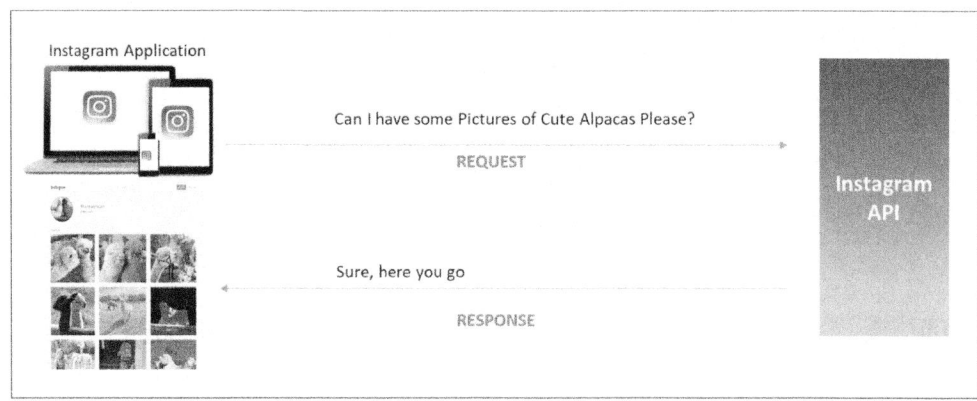

In order to do this, the following happens step by step:

- User Opens the App.

- User is bored with their current feed and pulls down to refresh the page or clicks the search/explore button (a trigger or action or API call)
- The parameters from the Instagram app are now sent to the servers
    - Parameters could include the search keywords or accounts the user is following, and the service sends this info to the servers on what the user needs. Here the API acts as a link between the database and the application on the user's phone.
    - Eg: "cute alpacas" which would have a unique ID for Instagram to search their database
- Servers then retrieve the information based on the parameters shared from user's application and send in a language called 'JSON'
    - Instagram will find the new info based on what the user asked for and will send it back to user's phone via the API
    - Given API documentation will detail out what the request should be and what should be expected in the response.
- Voila, new info on the screen

You now understand what a Request and Response is! Congratulations.

TYPES OF APIS

Dev.to defines these quite simply here. Overall, APIs are quite broad terminology and what we have been focusing on are Web service related APIs so far. (Because as users, we are more exposed to those).

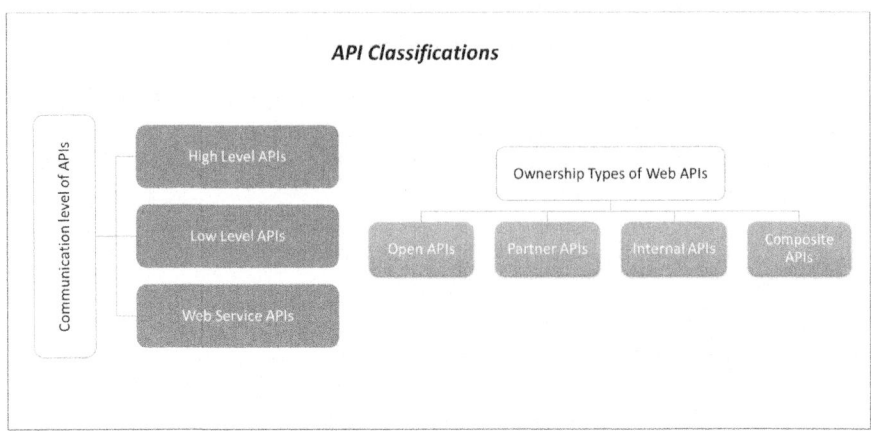

Nevertheless, high-level highlights will help. APIs Can be classified on the basis of the following Parameters.

- Ownership types of Web APIs
- Communication level of APIs

Ownership types of Web APIs

Based on their ownership type, APIs can be of four types:

- **Open APIs:**
  These are publicly available to use and there is no restriction to use them. These are also known as Public APIs. Open APIs might require registration from the user, and use of an API key, or in some instances might be completely open. They are meant for external users (developers at other organizations, for example) to access data or services to integrate with their products. There are tons of these that you can see for yourself. A few examples include https://openweathermap.org , https://thecocktaildb.com

In our use case of the Notes Application above, when you decided to create an API for third party apps to access notes, you could choose to create an Open API. This would allow any kind of application to access your notes (data).

- **Partner APIs:**
These require specific licenses or rights to be accessed and are not available to the public. These are often controlled through a gateway and are usually associated with paid services. Some of quite common services are like https://thecocktaildb.com (paid partnerships)

In our use case of the Notes Application above, when you had to create an API for third party apps to access notes, you could choose to create a Partner API. This would then require external applications to partner with you on a payment/license/authentication basis if they wanted to integrate your application in their products.

- **Internal APIs:**
APIs that are developed to be used internally by an organization to connect between different systems or products are called Internal APIs. These are also known as Private APIs. Eg: Your timesheets that automatically connect to your leave balance and payroll.

- **Composite APIs:**
Composite APIs combine many small APIs together to make one single call. In one single call multiple tasks run synchronously. Composite APIs come in handy when a user needs information from several different services to perform a single task. Benefits of using composite APIs include optimizing server load and improving application performance, as it would replace multiple API calls with one API call that can return all the data a user needs.

 Open https://www.marksandspencer.com/, **search for something and add it in your cart or wish list without logging in.**

In this example. You want to get the latest designer shoes. So you open the M&S site, search for them. Now you add these to your wish list. The moment you click the 'heart' it sends a composite API call -> this API creates an anonymous account in the background and adds these nice shoes in that wish list. So instead of doing these tasks separately with two APIs, these get done by one composite API.

Communication level of APIs

The other classification of APIs is by the level of communication:

Through these, one can classify the APIs into high-level and low level. This defines the level of change that needs to be made in an application for any functionality. High-level will mean limited changes or usage and low-level will mean detailed usage and impact.

- **High Level APIs**
  High-level APIs are where developers have a high level of abstraction; high-level API's are created for limited functionalities only. Their usage is pretty limited as per functionalities
- **Low Level APIs**
  Low-level APIs have a lower level of abstraction hence they are quite detailed, which allows the developer to modify functions within an application module or within hardware at a granular level. These are generally used when there is a need for detailed abstraction.
- **Web Service APIs**
  Web APIs are our focus. These are like tiny applications that use URLs or web addresses on the web to provide their services to desktop, mobile, web applications, and others.

As discussed earlier, we will keep our focus on web APIs for the purpose of this conversation.

WEB SERVICE APIS

A web service is something that is made available over the web. As the term suggests, web + services, and by definition, they work over a network. The term "web service" is defined pretty well by W3C (the World Wide Web Consortium) and it follows a set of standards. Here is a simpler version of the definition for Web Services:

> A Web service is a software component designed to support machine-to-machine interaction over a network with optimum interoperability. External or internal systems can interact with the Web service based on the standards or ways described using SOAP-messages, conveyed using HTTP.

APIs and web services are not mutually exclusive. As discussed above web services are a subset of the APIs and hence,

> *Every web service is an API, but not every API is a web service.*

Since we are almost always connected to the web, when we talk about APIs, we are referring to the web service APIs (APIs that are accessible over the internet). This is not always applicable. APIs can work without a network on local system. These APIs allow two local applications to talk to each other.

- Web services require a network. While APIs can work without a network too and can be either offline or online.
- APIs are protocol agnostic. While APIs can use any protocols or design styles, web services commonly use SOAP, REST, XML, JSON, UDDI, others

Web service APIs are classified in two ways. Based on the behavioral approach used in building the APIs and the type of communication.

- SOAP
- XML-RPC
- JSON-RPC
- REST

SOAP

SOAP, also known as Simple Object Access Protocol is a web services access protocol that was originally developed by Microsoft, SOAP is the most commonly used messaging protocol for exchanging information between two computers over the web in XML. SOAP messages are written in XML and are platform and language independent.

A SOAP message contains:

- A message format that indicates the start and end of the message
- A Header that has the attributes used to process the message. This is an optional element
- A Body which is the main component, that holds the XML data
- A Fault which gives details of error messages when processing

JSON-RPC and XML-RPC

An RPC is a remote procedural call protocol. JSON-RPC uses JSON to encode their calls, and XML-RPC uses XML to encode their calls. XML-RPC and JSON-RPC are not used widely, but SOAP is pretty widely used especially for of financial services and corporates like Salesforce.

A RPC, remote procedural call can contain multiple parameters, and expects one result. They have a couple of key features, which require a different architecture to REST (described below)

REST

REST (Representational State Transfer) is another standard for web service APIs and is most commonly heard about and used these days. This was made in response to SOAP's shortcomings. REST resolves some issues that persist with SOAP and help with a simpler method of accessing web services. REST is used to describe a set of architectural principles and characteristics outlined which should be followed in order to create a RESTful API.

EXAMPLE 💡 Let us visualize it this way, If you were having a theme party, you would have a few standard rules for the guests to come, like a dress code, maybe red and black. REST is those set of rules (wearing red or black) that developers should follow while creating the RESTful API (entering your party).

We will not get into further details, as these can get quite technical. REST helps to standardize APIs, so a developer doesn't need to learn multiple standards for each individual APIs. If you are working with RESTful APIs, the standards will be the same. Also, REST APIs all use the same HTTP Methods.

COMMON HTTP METHODS (REST)

Methods or verbs are the ways to do things with APIs.

 **If you were in a soccer team and had secret formations, you and your team would create codes/keywords for those. Could be Code1, Code2, Code3. Based on when you use these codes, the team would rearrange in a certain way, or ACT based on the codes.**

Methods are similar, they tell the API in code/keywords what needs to be done or how to ACT. Here's a summary of these:

POST	Used to create new resources.
	For example, if we wanted to create a new user profile in Instagram, we would use the POST method since this is how you create new resources (where the resource is the profile).
GET	Used to read / fetch a representation of a resource. When the GET method is used, the response contains the information requested. GET requests are used to read data and not modify it.
	For example, in the Instagram example, GET is used to retrieve or Get a list of posts from the database.
PUT	Used to update / replace data.
	For example, updating all the details in a user profile
DELETE	Self-explanatory. Used to delete data.

Of course, there are others but we are only going to focus on these since these are the most common. If you know these, you know enough. One more term that comes in handy is the "Endpoint"

ENDPOINT

It's a connection point (a URL/link/Web address) which accepts requests to access resources on an API. Commonly used Terminology:

"Hit an endpoint"

"Expose endpoint"

"Call an endpoint"

 **Getting back to our waffle example. For the sake of reference, let's name the restaurant 'Waffle Bar' which had a delicious breakfast menu. If you were to ever visit this restaurant, you would need their address. That address or the destination is the ENDPOINT. Let's look at the HTTP methods with this example.**

GET

On a nice Sunday afternoon, you entered the 'Waffle Bar' and requested the waiter to get the menu. That's it. That's a METHOD: GET.

Here you REQUESTed the waiter to GET the menu. Let's see what the GET method would like for 'waffle Bar'

Endpoint: wafflebar.com/Menu?itemtype=All

Method: Get

Request Body: None

Response Body:
```
{
 "data": [{
"itemtype": "waffles",
"items": [

{
 "name": "Waffles",
 "price": "$5.95",
 "description": "two Waffles with chocolate syrup",
 "Calories": "650",
},
{
 "name": "strawberry Waffles",
 "price": "$7.95",
 "description": "light Waffles with blueberries and cream",
 "Calories": "900",
 }
]
},
"Itemtype": "sides",
 "sides": [
   {
     "name": "sausage",
     "price": "$2.00"
   },
   {
     "type": "bacon",
     "number": "$2.50"
   }
  ]
},
]}
```

POST

You now love the waffles at the Waffle Bar, but don't love their sides and would like to have some fries. But of course Waffle Bar does not have fries on their menu. What you could do is make a custom request of fries. The chef thinks that this was a valid request and that this could work well for "waffle bar". The chef not just gives you fries but also adds this to their menu.

This method or request type is called POST.

Request: The chef will request to add 'Fries' on the menu. The request should contain the item name that needs to be added along with other details.
Response: The outcome would be to see the confirmation that 'Fries' is added on the menu.

Endpoint: wafflebar.com/newside/
Method: Post
Request Body:
{
'Content-Type': application/json'
'Accept': application/json'
'Data': {
        'itemtype': 'side',
    'name' : 'fries',
    'price': '$2.50'
              }
}
Response Body:
HTTP/1.1 200 OK
Content-Type: application/jsonrequest

PUT

Now, fries are already a big hit the waffle bar, but the chef thinks he is at loss and decides to update the price for fries.

Request: The chef thinks of a new price and wants the same to be updated for the item 'Fries'. The request should have the reference of the item that needs to be updated and the parameters that need the update along with the values.

Response: The outcome would be to see the updated price in the menu for 'Fries'.

Endpoint: wafflebar.com/menu/

Method: Put

Request Body:

{

'Content-Type': application/json'

'Accept': application/json'

'Data': {

      'itemtype': 'side',

    'name' : 'fries',

    'price': '$3.50'

      }

}

Response Body:

HTTP/1.1 200 OK

Content-Type: application/jsonrequest

DELETE

With the increased demand from fries, the chef thinks, he should remove bacon from the menu.

The act of removing is called Delete.

Request: The chef will request to remove 'Bacon' from the menu. The request should have the item name amongst other details that needs to be removed from the menu.

Response: The outcome would be to see the confirmation that 'Bacon' is no longer visible on the menu.

Endpoint: wafflebar.com/menu/itemType=side/name='bacon'

Method:Delete

Response Body:

HTTP/1.1 200 OK

Content-Type: application/jsonrequest

These are great examples. However, the APIs don't always work and just like our brains have a writer's block, the APIs may not always respond favorably. Fortunately, there's set standard of response codes to decode the APIs moody behavior as well.

RESPONSE CODES

Every time an API sends a response, it comes with its own response code, which is simply a number with ax explanation attached to it.

2xx	Means that the request was successful.
3xx	Imagine you go to the imaginary "Waffle Bar", only to find a notice that says it has moved to a new address and the new directions written over there. This code means that the request is redirected to a different URL.
4xx	You for to the "Waffle Bar" to get some waffles and bacon as a side. But the bacon is no longer served in the waffle bar. This is equivalent to the client side errors like age not found, unauthorized, forbidden.
5xx	You went to the Waffle Bar during holidays. You ordered your favorite waffles, but everyone was ordering the same, and it took a while to get your order. Meanwhile, you left the waffle bar. In API terminology, it means either gateway timeout or Service not available.

There are many other response codes but these are most common response codes. Now, when people talk about 'a 500' you will know it's a problem with the server. For some fun reference on response codes, check https://http.cat/

2xx Successful Requests	3xx Redirects	4xx Client Errors	5xx Server Errors
200 OK – Request was successful.	300 Multiple Choices	400 Bad Request	500 Internal Server Error
201 Created	301 Moved Permanently	401 Unauthorized	501 Not Implemented –
202 Accepted	302 Found	403 Forbidden	502 Bad Gateway
203 Non-authoritative Information	303 See Other (HTTP/1.1)	404 Not Found	503 Service Unavailable
204 No Content	304 Not Modified	405 Method Not Allowed	504 Gateway Timeout
205 Reset Content	305 Use Proxy	406 Not Acceptable	505 HTTP Version Not Supported
206 Partial Content –	307 Temporary Redirect (HTTP/1.1)	407 Proxy Authentication Required	
		408 Request Timeout	
		409 Conflict	
		410 Gone	
		411 Length Required	
		412 Precondition Failed	
		413 Request Entity Too Large	
		414 Request URI Too Long	
		415 Unsupported Media Type	
		416 Requested Range Not Satisfiable	
		417 Expectation Failed	

API DOCUMENTATION

API documentation is key to many facets of an API. It is a crucial document that helps product managers understand the capability of an API, the feasibility of integration and eventually in making decisions.

Understanding, creating, validating API Documentation is a great skillset to possess.

The documentation contains instructions on how to use and integrate with an API. It's a straightforward manual containing as much information as possible that is required to work with the API. It could contain details about the functions, classes, return types, arguments, step-by-step usage guides and more, supported by examples.

 Let's see some examples for API documentation

Twilio – A lot of folks have been talking about the way Twilio has detailed this out and it truly is outstanding. Their documentation is in three columns – navigation, explanation, and code. Its structured, clear and well-thought-through. The left-most column provides a clear overview of the topics and makes it easy to find the content. All of the info rests in the central pane with details. The right-most column gives details via code-snippets and live examples. They have also broken this down by coding language. Users can select their coding language and choose the code of their choice to work with the API.

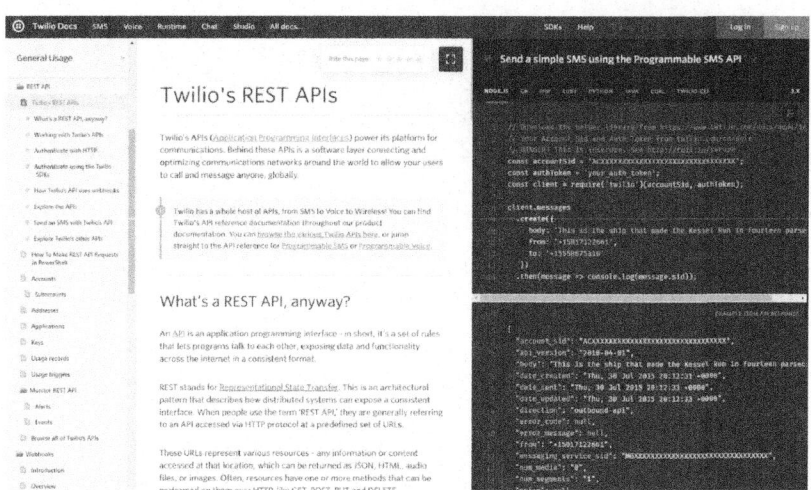

Another example is Instagram API. Take a look

Types of API Documentation

There are three major types of API documentation: conceptual documentation, reference documentation and tutorials.

Let's take a look at the Google REST API Documentation

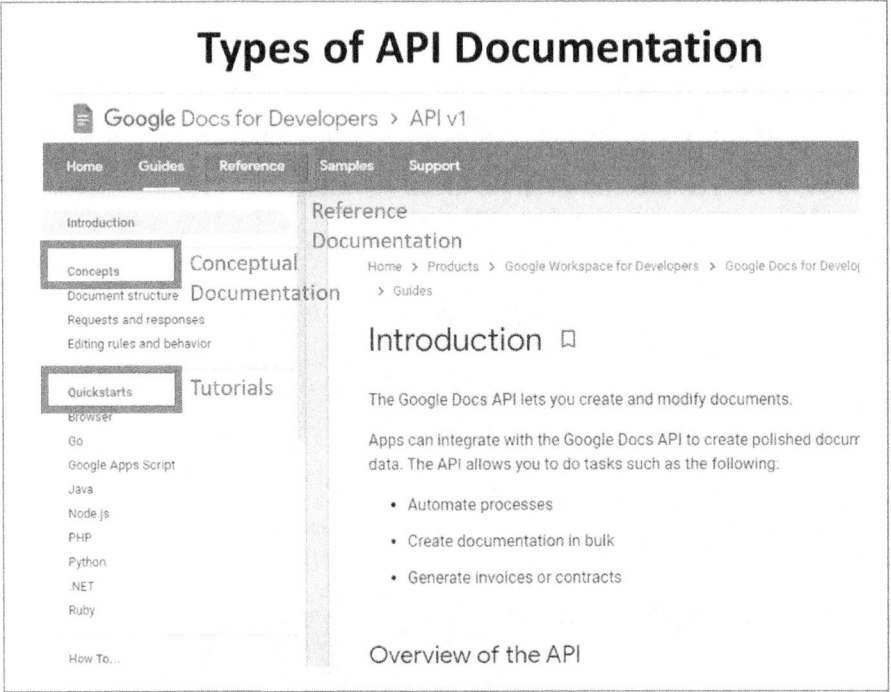

- **Conceptual documentation** is the main crux of API documentation. It provides a high-level understanding of the API overall and its capabilities. This may also include information and sample cases on integrating multiple APIs in one application.
- **Reference documentation** provides details on each component like the structure, parameters, and response values. It is only one aspect of the overall documentation.
- **Tutorials** break down the overall usage of an API into step-by-step instructions. They contain examples of specific tasks with detailed explanations of parameters and endpoints.

API Documentation Structure

Documentation is the key to a great experience when exploring an API and making key business decisions related to the API. It enables the user to understand the right intention behind the API and the possible scope upfront.

We will focus on REST APIs for the purpose of this section. In any API documentation, there are familiar terms, commonly used across most APIs. Linking back to what we learned with REST, it's a benefit of using the REST principles; REST APIs make use of common methods, which makes it easier to integrate into multiple APIs.

There could be many ways to create an API documentation. A standard practice would include most of the following in an API documentation:

Authentication instructions	How to connect with the API
API endpoints	What endpoints are available
Resources	What resources are available to access. For example in the Instagram API, they allow to you access basic profile information, photos, and videos
Request format	How an HTTP request should be formatted
Respone format	How an HTTP response is formatted
Response codes	What response codes are included in the response

If you had to structure an API documentation, a good practice would be to have at least the following elements included:

- Authentication Guide
- Quickstart guide
- Endpoint definitions
- Code snippets
- Example responses

Many commercial platforms like SwaggerHub and open source description formats like OpenAPI Specification allow teams to automate the documentation process. This in turn provides a great overall experience consuming APIs. There are many API calling tools like POSTMAN, which create documentation automatically. They are an excellent way for simplifying the documentation process and kick starting your journey.

WORK WITH AN API (LIVE EXAMPLE)

All this theory is not a lot of value if you are not able to use it.

 We will work with https://restcountries.eu Visit the site, read their documentation and scroll around to see what's available.

It's quite straightforward. There's no specific functionality on the website as it is made purely from an API perspective. Scrolling down you'll see the ALL section.

NAME

Search by country name. It can be the native name or partial name

https://restcountries.eu/rest/v2/name/{name}

https://restcountries.eu/rest/v2/name/eesti

https://restcountries.eu/rest/v2/name/united

If you copy the first link, you can see it includes the location name and a couple of other parameters.

https://restcountries.eu/rest/v2/name/{name}

If you paste this URL in a different tab in the browser as it is and hit Enter. What do you get?

{"status":404,"message":"Not Found"}

We did cover response codes earlier. So, Scroll up to see what '404' means.

Now, let's try to use the API in the browser. Add any country name that you like in the parentheses {} which generally denotes value of a parameter to be added. I am choosing Greenland, because I'm utterly bored caged indoors due to the pandemic and the word 'Greenland' itself brings flutters to the soul.

https://restcountries.eu/rest/v2/name/greenland

Hit Enter.

What happens?

You get a response. This is what it looks like:

[{"name":"Greenland","topLevelDomain":[".gl"],"alpha2Code":"GL","alpha3Code":"GRL","callingCodes":["299"],"capital":"Nuuk","altSpellings":["GL","Grønland"],"region":"Americas","subregion":"Northern America","population":55847,"latlng":[72.0,-40.0],"demonym":"Greenlandic","area":2166086.0,"gini":null,"timezones":["UTC-04:00","UTC-03:00","UTC-01:00","UTC+00:00"],"borders":[],"nativeName":"Kalaallit Nunaat","numericCode":"304","currencies":[{"code":"DKK","name":"Danish krone","symbol":"kr"}],"languages":[{"iso639_1":"kl","iso639_2":"kal","name":"Kalaallisut","nativeName":"kalaallisut"}],"translations":{"de":"Grönland","es":"Groenlandia","fr":"Groenland","ja":"グリーンランド","it":"Groenlandia","br":"Groelândia","pt":"Gronelândia","nl":"Groenland","hr":"Grenland","fa":"گرینلند"},"flag":"https://restcountries.eu/data/grl.svg","regionalBlocs":[],"cioc":""}]

Now, Now, there's no need to panic. Because we know what XML and JSON look like already, this is just unstructured JSON. If we format this a little differently or use some online tools to format this data, it starts to make sense.

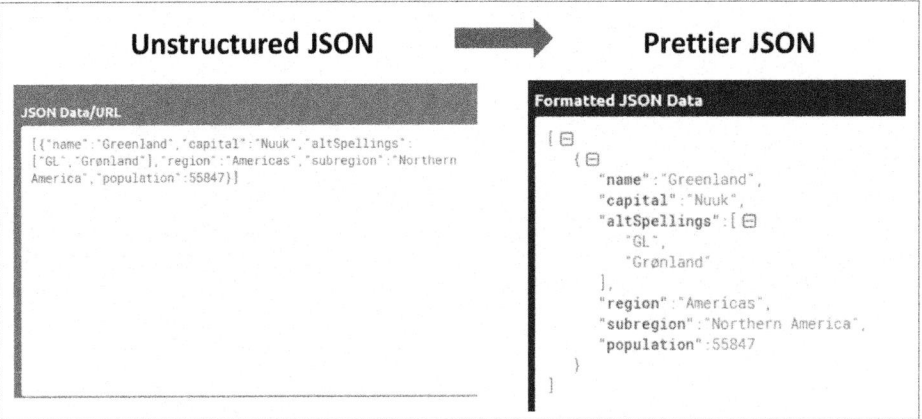

Let see the above code in prettier JSON.

```
[{
    "name":"Greenland",
    "topLevelDomain":[".gl"],
    "alpha2Code":"GL",
    "alpha3Code":"GRL",
    "callingCodes":["299"],
    "capital":"Nuuk",
    "altSpellings":["GL","Grønland"],
    "region":"Americas",
    "subregion":"NorthernAmerica",
    "Population":55847,
    "LatIng":[72.0,-40.0],
    "demonym":"Greenlandic",
    "Area":2166086.0,
    "Gini":null,
    "Timezones":["UTC-04:00", "UTC-03:00","UTC-01:00","UTC+00:00"],
    "Borders":[],
    "nativeName":"Kalaallit Nunaat",
    "numericCode":"304",
    "Currencies":[{
        "code":"DKK",
        "name":"Danishkrone",
        "Symbol":"kr"
    }],
    "Languages":[{
        "Iso639_1":"kl",
        "Iso639_2":"kal",
        "name":"Kalaallisut",
        "nativeName":"kalaallisut"
    }],
    "Translations":{
        "de":"Grönland",
        "es":"Groenlandia",
        "fr":"Groenland",
        "Ja":"グリーンランド",
        "it":"Groenlandia",
        "br":"Groelândia",
        "pt":"Gronelândia",
        "nl":"Groenland",
        "hr":"Grenland",
        "Fa":"گرینلند"
    },
    "flag":"https://restcountries.eu/data/grl.svg",
    "regionalBlocs":[],
    "Cioc":""
}]
```

The reply from the API is a data structure with information about the country. Every time you type the country name and press enter, the website connects to a server with a specific link which includes the name of the country as a parameter.

As you read the documentation, you can see that the API allows you to search by various other combinations like country codes, capital city, regions etc. Go ahead give it a try.

There are several other fun websites you could try. Let's take another example:

**Let's take another example** https://openweathermap.org/ . **Here we will do a slight dev work to get to the API response. Or we could directly look at the API documentation** https://openweathermap.org/api

- Open the link in Chrome
- In Chrome click on the top 3 dots and choose -> More Tools -> Developer Tools
- It opens up a tab on the right side of the window. Click on the Network tab.
- Your screen will look like this:

- Now let's search for weather in any city.
- I am going to check on Greenland just because. Before you hit search, watch the right pane.
- While it searches for your data, it sends some parameters via URL to search for the data, this gets populated in the right panel.

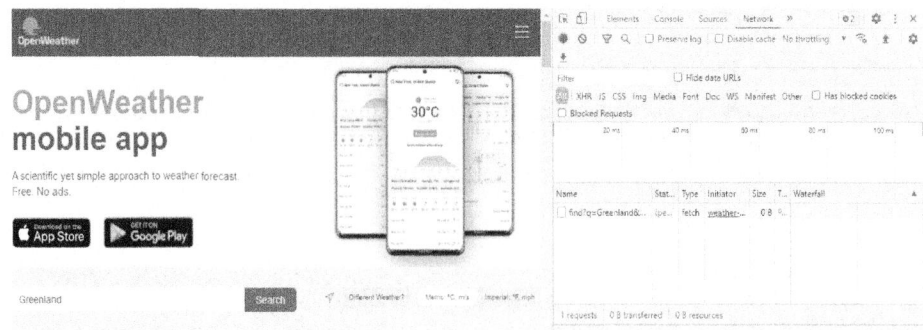

- Let's copy this and paste in a new tab. Hit enter
- The URL Looks like this:
  https://openweathermap.org/data/2.5/find?q=Greenland&appid=439d4b804bc8187953eb36d2a8c26a02&units=metric
- What happens once you hit enter?
- It gives you a response.

{"message":"accurate","cod":"200","count":3,"list":[{"id":5086915,"name":"Greenland","coord":{"lat":43.0362,"lon":-70.8323},"main":{"temp":293.93,"feels_like":294.26,"temp_min":292.51,"temp_max":295.44,"pressure":1019,"humidity":84},"dt":1626516578,"wind":{"speed":1.54,"deg":30},"sys":{"country":"US"},"rain":null,"snow":null,"clouds":{"all":90},"weather":[{"id":804,"main":"Clouds","description":"overcast clouds","icon":"04d"}]},{"id":4113113,"name":"Greenland","coord":{"lat":35.9943,"lon":-94.1752},"main":{"temp":295.25,"feels_like":295.94,"temp_min":292.91,"temp_max":296.14,"pressure":1018,"humidity":93},"dt":1626516770,"wind":{"speed":2.57,"deg":160},"sys":{"country":"US"},"rain":{"1h":1.55},"snow":null,"clouds":{"all":90},"weather":[{"id":501,"main":"Rain","description":"moderate rain","icon":"10n"},{"id":701,"main":"Mist","description":"mist","icon":"50n"}]},{"id":3425505,"name":"Greenland","coord":{"lat":72,"lon":-40},"main":{"temp":262.38,"feels_like":255.38,"temp_min":262.38,"temp_max":262.38,"pressure":1021,"humidity":79,"sea_level":1021,"grnd_level":692},"dt":1626516595,"wind":{"speed":7.5,"deg":230},"sys":{"country":"GL"},"rain":null,"snow":null,"clouds":{"all":80},"weather":[{"id":803,"main":"Clouds","description":"broken clouds","icon":"04n"}]}]}

If you structure this, it'll make more sense:

{
"message":"accurate",
"cod":"200",
"count":3,
"list":[
  {
    "id":5086915,

```
    "name":"Greenland",
    "coord":{
      "lat":43.0362,  "lon":-70.8328
    },
    "main":{
      "temp":293.93,
      "feels_like":294.26,
      "temp_min":292.51,
      "temp_max":295.44,
      "pressure":1019,
      "humidity":84
    },
    "dt":1626516578,
    "wind":{
      "speed":1.54, "deg":30
    },
    "sys":{
      "country":"US"
    },
    "rain":null, "snow":null, "clouds":{
      "all":90
    },
    "weather":[
      {
        "id":804,
        "main":"Clouds",
        "description":"overcast clouds",
        "icon":"04d"
      }
    ]
  },
```

There are many online tools that help a Product Managers and others to test the APIs and verify Documentation. The most common is Postman and its almost offensive to not talk about it while talking about APIs

 **API Testing & Documentation with POSTMAN**

- Log on to www.postman.com

- Once you are setup, this is the screen you'll see:

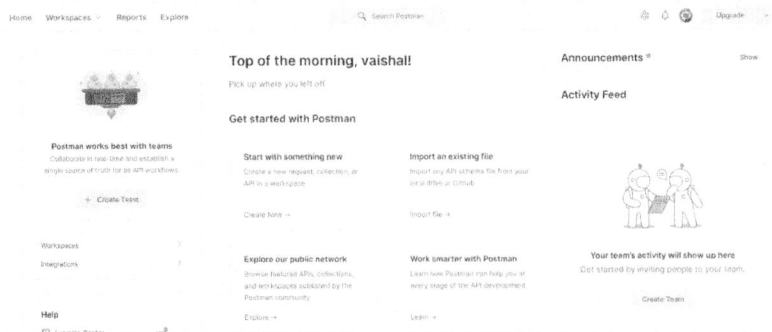

- Click on Create New under Start with Something new

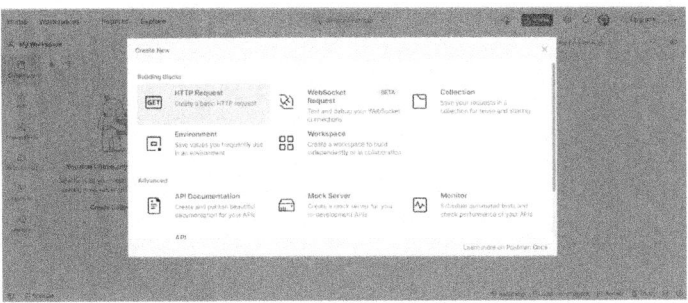

- Next Click on HTTP Request
- Once you land here, it's your playing field. Use any of the above URLs or examples for GET responses
- You can ask your dev teams to load the APIs in Postman for you to be able to test them. Also, you can easily create auto documentation and edit those via Postman.

Hope you got an idea of how an API works. There are other APIs you could experiment with and I've added a fun list in the end.

OTHER API TERMINOLOGIES

Here's a quick check of a few other terminologies that are commonly used with respect to APIs

API Calls

The requests from the Request-Response cycle are referred to as API calls.

API calls involve hitting an endpoint with the expectation that the API will respond with the information requested via the call. In the Instagram example, you call the posts endpoint with a specific search keyword "Cute Alpacas" and Instagram responds with the information.

Payloads

The response from the Request-Response cycle are referred to as payloads. Payload specifically refers to the important parameters in the given set of data. Sometimes there might be many parameters in a response and there may be only a few we care about. In this case, payload is used to differentiate between the stuff we're interested in and the stuff we're not.

E.g. 'If you check the payload from the restcountries.eu API you can see the population of Greenland is 55847'

Headers

In a Request-response cycle, both requests and responses contain headers.

Headers contain useful information and are sent and received along with the HTTP methods. Some headers are mandatory and some are rarely used.

Some of the most common headers are:

- Authorization – the authorization / authentication credentials such as username and password
- Content-type – this tells you how the information is sent in the response and what content is used. JSON, XML could be the languages used.
- Date – represents the date and timestamp of a request or a response.

In our waffle bar example, we saw:

HTTP/1.1 200 OK

Content-Type: application/jsonrequest

Authentication

Not all APIs would always be open to public. In many cases, product managers would want only agreed upon parties to be able to access the data via your product/product APIs.

In such scenarios, your request would have an identity to tell the API that your request is a genuine request made by a bona fide user who has the necessary privileges to access the API.

For this, the access for the API is set up using an authentication token. This is just like logging in to any email or social media via either password or an OTP.

If you have an external facing API that has to be accessed by clients, they will be issued a security token and credentials to access the API.

Authentication and authorization are not same:

- Authentication – proves WHO the user is
- Authorization – defines WHAT you are permitted, or authorized to do

Authentication usually includes:

- Username
- Password
- Access token

OAuth

OAuth is an authorization framework that can be used to authenticate and authorize users. Using OAuth involves a separate authentication server, which authenticates the user and then passes the details back to the resource API.

API TESTING & MONITORING

You got your API. Whether you integrated a third party API, Build an internal API or an external API, you should be done. But it is just the start.

What happens if the server goes out? Users are getting stranded when they try to send you information. There's delay in responses and your potential customers are looking for other services.

This is where monitoring comes in. API monitoring helps to check how the internal and third-party APIs are running. If there is a problem with a given API, monitoring will tell you the details. This will also allow your team to be on standby to fix the issues. In fact, with preemptive API monitoring, you should know about the problem beforehand and save it from impacting your customers at all. So they won't even notice it.

From a product perspective here are some Best Practices one could follow:

- **Monitor 24x7**
  Services go down when you're not looking, so having continuous monitoring is essential – 24/7 365 days a year, have all of your API endpoints tested by an external call.

- **Monitor Everything**
  Keep looking at every process, whether rarely used or often used. Sometimes issues with the rarely used resources will surface only when a user tries to use them. Like if a timesheet API went down on Monday and the team only realized when people filled their timesheet on a Friday; that would cause immense pain. But could have been prevented if the API was monitored throughout.

API Testing and why should you care?

Before you make the final business decision to integrate a third party API. Ensure the API does what it says and will work well with your product. You should test the various components of the API both directly and in action with the site itself. A quick list of things to test would include:

- The functionality of the API
- Do the described API functions makes business sense
- The API load are comparable to the business expectations
- Runtime error tests
- Security testing
- WS compliance testing
- Interoperability testing

BONUS

List of fun APIs

- NASA Open APIs
  NASA has a set of super exciting APIs for the public. One of the APIs called Astronomy Picture of the Day send a new picture from space each day. There are other APIs that get the weather on Mars, and just for Mars Rover photos. Definite yes to check these out.
- Agify API
  Agify API tries to predict the user's age from their name. API key is not needed and one can just send a request with name in it to find out what their algorithm thinks of the user age
- The Bored API
  If you are bored during the pandemic, have fun with this. When you send the Bored API a request, it sends back a fun activity.
- Fun Translation API
  Fun Translations API allows to use several fun language APIs under one plan. Some of the many language APIs include the Yoda API, which translates English to Yodish, a Pig Latin API, and an API to translate Dothraki (from Game of Thrones)
- Eventbrite API
  This simple API lets you find different events and information about them, like their capacity, pricing, and more
- Coinbase API
  With a focus on cryptocurrency, their API can be used to check the price of cryptocurrency, to buy it, and more

REFERENCES

https://www.departmentofproduct.com/blog/apis-explained-for-product-managers/

https://uxdesign.cc/decoding-apis-in-simple-terms-for-product-managers-e93723a6e589

https://http.cat

https://www.smashingmagazine.com/2019/01/api-based-platforms-product-managers/

https://www.citigroup.com/citi/news/2021/210412b.htm

https://stoplight.io/api-types/)

https://www.authoritylabs.com/common-http-response-codes-and-what-they-mean/

PHEW, I KNOW ENOUGH - WHAT TO DO WITH THIS INFO?

You are ready to take the API matters in your hands and fight the API battles with vendors, stakeholders, Dev teams. Experiment with several open APIs.

1. Experiment with suggested APIs if you haven't already. Take inspiration from above described Live examples and get ahead
2. Look at APIs from various products that you use on a daily basis and try to analyze what type, structure they follow.
3. API documentation is key, so try to create sample documentation, read other API documentations and learn as you go.

Thank you,
Pallavi Agarwal

> Hope you found this useful. Do not forget to share your feedback or say hello at producthumour@gmail.com
>
> Join our Product Community on Instagram: https://www.instagram.com/producthumour
> Read other helpful articles: https://medium.com/@agarwalpallavi

Printed in Great Britain
by Amazon